UNOFFICIAL
**GUIDES**
JUNIOR

# Starter Guide to
# Pokémon

by Josh Gregory

CHERRY LAKE PRESS
Ann Arbor, Michigan

Published in the United States of America by Cherry Lake Publishing
Ann Arbor, Michigan
www.cherrylakepublishing.com

Reading Adviser: Beth Walker Gambro, MS, Ed., Reading Consultant, Yorkville, IL

Photo Credits: Images by Josh Gregory

**Cherry Lake Press** is an imprint of Cherry Lake Publishing Group.

Library of Congress Cataloging-in-Publication Data has been filed and is available at catalog.loc.gov

Printed in the United States of America by
Corporate Graphics

Note from the Publisher: Websites change regularly, and their future contents are outside of our control. Supervise children when conducting any recommended online searches for extended learning opportunities.

# Contents

Pokémon Is Everywhere! .............4

Ways to Play .......................6

Pick a Game .......................8

Gotta Catch 'Em All! ...............10

Catching a Pokémon ...............12

Poké Balls ........................14

Changing Pokémon ................16

Battling ..........................18

What's Next?......................20

Glossary ....................................22

Find Out More ...............................23

Index .......................................24

About the Author ............................24

# Pokémon Is Everywhere!

The first Pokémon video game was created in Japan in 1996.

Look around. Pokémon is everywhere. There are Pokémon TV shows and movies. There are card games, toys, and comic books! Did you know the Pokémon craze all started with a video game about collecting little pocket monsters? Today, there are dozens of games in the Pokémon **series**. Are you ready to explore the games for yourself?

## A Very Popular Game

Altogether, hundreds of millions of people play Pokémon. And Pokémon mobile apps have been downloaded more than 1 billion times!

# Ways to Play

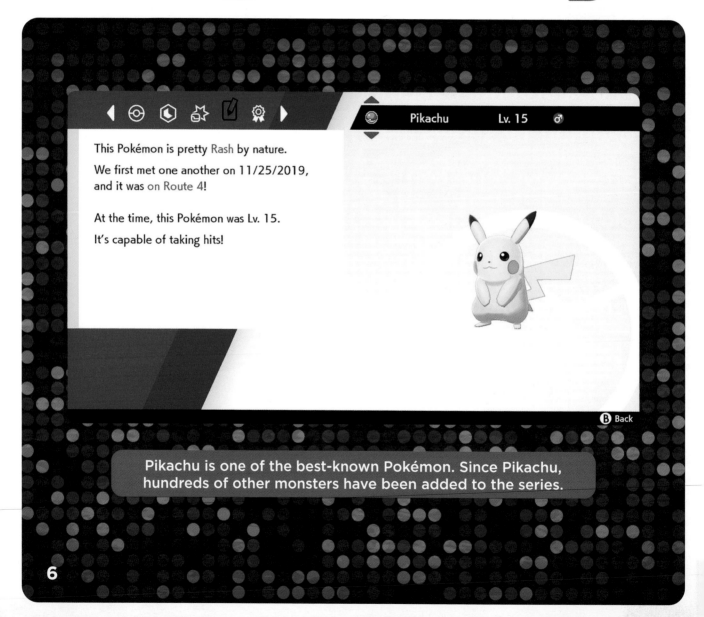

This Pokémon is pretty Rash by nature.

We first met one another on 11/25/2019, and it was on Route 4!

At the time, this Pokémon was Lv. 15.

It's capable of taking hits!

Pikachu        Lv. 15

Ⓑ Back

Pikachu is one of the best-known Pokémon. Since Pikachu, hundreds of other monsters have been added to the series.

The main Pokémon series is made up of **roleplaying games** (RPGs). To play, you become a Pokémon trainer. Your mission is to catch Pokémon! Pokémon are small monsters that battle other monsters. Each one has different strengths. Trainers help the creatures grow. They also battle other trainers. The goal is to be the best trainer!

# Pick a Game

Pokémon Sword and Pokémon Shield also have open-world areas for players to explore.

Which Pokémon game should you play? Choose one for your gaming system. Each game will help you learn about the world of Pokémon. In 2022, *Pokémon Scarlet* and *Pokémon Violet* were released. They allowed players to wander around freely to find new Pokémon. Fans were thrilled to try it out.

## Generations

Pokémon games are released 2 or 3 at a time. Each game has different Pokémon. These sets are called "generations" or "gens." The first generation included *Pokémon Red, Pokémon Blue*, and *Pokémon Yellow*. They were released in 1996.

# Gotta Catch 'Em All!

Filling in the Pokédex is a fun part of the game.

Catching new Pokémon is a big part of every game. For each Pokémon you find, you will unlock another entry in your Pokédex. A Pokédex is like a Pokémon **encyclopedia**. It is something your Pokémon trainer character carries around. Your goal is to complete the entire Pokédex!

# Catching a Pokémon

Pokémon live in many different places. A player can hunt some Pokémon by sneaking up on them.

There are more than 1,000 different Pokémon to catch. So how do you catch one? First, you need to find a wild Pokémon. When you come across one, you need to battle it. Using the Pokémon you already have, you can attack the wild Pokémon. Once you've weakened it, you can throw a Poké Ball at it.

## Battle with Caution

Be sure not to attack the Pokémon too much. It is a sensitive creature. If you cause it to faint, the battle will be over!

# Poké Balls

Gotcha!
Rookidee was caught!

Red-and-white Poké Balls work to capture some Pokémon.
However, sometimes more powerful Poké Balls are needed.

A Poké Ball can be used to trap a Pokémon inside. If the tool works, the wild Pokémon will be yours. You can raise it and use it in battles. However, Poké Balls don't always work. Some Pokémon are tough to catch. They need to be captured with other methods.

# Changing Pokémon

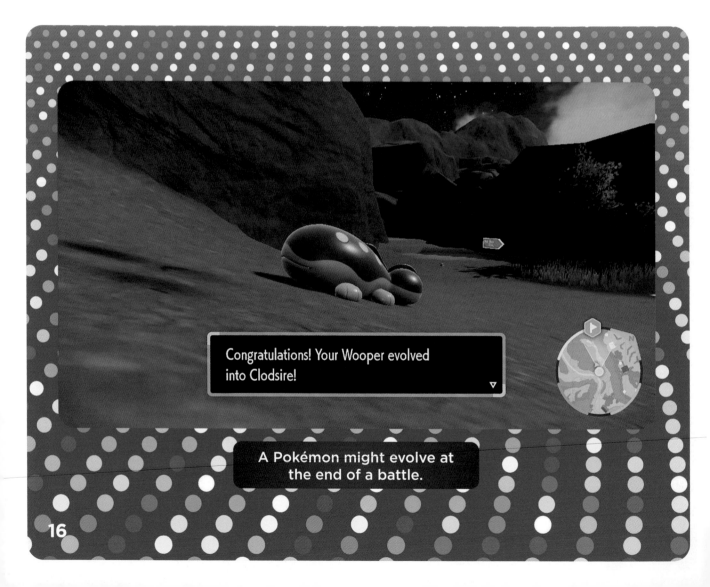

Congratulations! Your Wooper evolved into Clodsire!

A Pokémon might evolve at the end of a battle.

Some Pokémon cannot be caught in the wild. You will have to try another way! For example, there are Pokémon that evolve into other Pokémon. They might turn into new **species** at a certain level. Others evolve when you give them items. For example, if you let Pikachu hold a Thunderstone, it will **evolve** into Raichu.

## Pokémon Eggs

Some Pokémon can create eggs together. These eggs can then hatch into new monsters!

# Battling

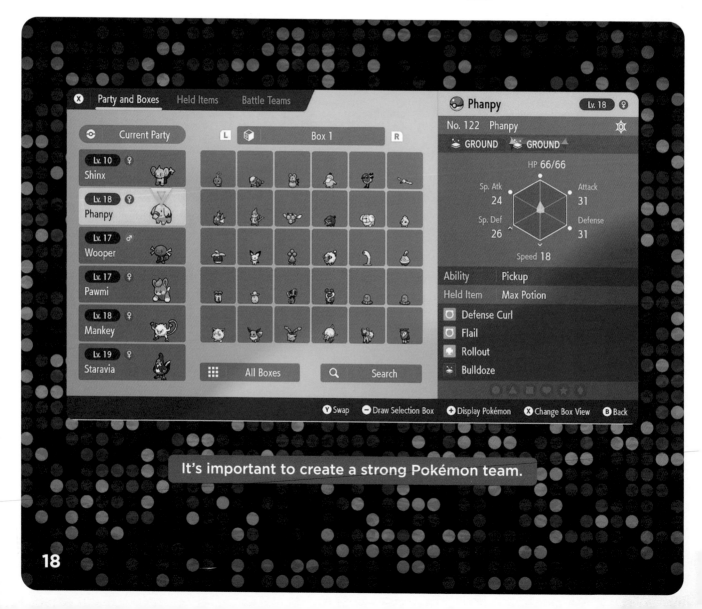

It's important to create a strong Pokémon team.

Once you've collected your Pokémon, you can battle them! Players enjoy training their Pokémon to have certain skills. Each Pokémon has a "type," such as electric or ice. Some types are better at battling other types. Each Pokémon has **stats** that show its strengths and weaknesses.

## Trading and Keeping Pokémon

You can also get new Pokémon by trading with other players. Also, Nintendo has created apps that allow you to keep your Pokémon from each game. One is called Pokémon Home.

# What's Next?

It's time to start exploring the world of Pokémon!

Pokémon will continue to evolve. No matter how you play, there's always something new to learn. So start capturing your own team of colorful creatures. Get out there and battle. Challenge other players. You'll be a top trainer in no time!

# GLOSSARY

**encyclopedia** (en-sahy-kluh-PEE-dee-uh) a resource containing a lot of information on various topics

**evolve** (i-VOLV) to change over time

**roleplaying games** (ROHL-play-ing GAYMZ) games in which the player builds and strengthens a character or set of characters

**series** (SIHR-eez) a set of games

**species** (SPEE-sheez) a certain kind of something

**stats** (STATS) numerical measurements of different strengths and weaknesses

# FIND OUT MORE

## BOOKS

Gregory, Josh. *Careers in Esports*. Ann Arbor, MI: Cherry Lake Publishing, 2021.

Loh-Hagan, Virginia. *Video Games. In the Know: Influencers and Trends*. Ann Arbor, MI: 45th Parallel Press, 2021.

Orr, Tamra. *Video Sharing. Global Citizens: Social Media*. Ann Arbor, MI: Cherry Lake Press, 2019.

Reeves, Diane Lindsey. *Do You Like Getting Creative? Career Clues for Kids*. Ann Arbor, MI: Cherry Lake Press, 2023.

## WEBSITES

With an adult, learn more online with these suggested searches:

### The Official Pokémon Website
Keep up to date with all of the latest Pokémon news at the series' official website.

### Bulbapedia
You'll find detailed information about all of the Pokémon games at this fan-created wiki site.

# INDEX

battles, 7, 13, 15, 16, 18–19, 21

catching Pokémon, 10–15, 21
changing Pokémon, 16–17

eggs, 17
evolution, 16–17, 21

gameplay descriptions, 7, 8–21
gameplay options, 5, 19
generations, 9
graphics, 4, 6, 8, 12, 14, 16, 18, 20

Pikachu, 6, 17
Poké Balls, 13, 14–15
Pokédex, 10–11
Pokémon brand, 4–5, 19, 20–21

Pokémon characters, 6, 7, 10–11, 12–13,
  16–17, 18–19
Pokémon *Red, Blue, and Yellow*, 9
Pokémon *Scarlet*, 9
Pokémon *Shield*, 8
Pokémon *Sword*, 8
Pokémon *Violet*, 9
popularity, 4–5

Raichu, 17
roleplaying games, 7, 8–9

trading Pokémon, 19
training Pokémon, 7, 19, 21

wild Pokémon, 12–13, 14–15

# ABOUT THE AUTHOR

**Josh Gregory** is the author of more than 200 books for kids. He has written about everything from animals to technology to history. A graduate of the University of Missouri–Columbia, he currently lives in Chicago, Illinois.